religion in focus
judaism

Geoff Teece

First published in 2003 by Franklin Watts
Franklin Watts, 96 Leonard Street, London EC2A 4XD

Franklin Watts Australia
45–51 Huntley Street, Alexandria, NSW 2015
This edition published under license from Franklin Watts. All rights reserved.

Copyright © 2003 Franklin Watts

Series Editor: Adrian Cole; Designer: Proof Books; Art Director: Jonathan Hair; Consultant: Jonathan Gorsky, The Council of Christians and Jews; Picture Researcher: Diana Morris

Published in the United States by Smart Apple Media
1980 Lookout Drive, North Mankato, Minnesota 56003

Library of Congress Cataloging-in-Publication Data

Teece, Geoff.
Judaism / Geoff Teece.
p. col. ill. cm. — (Religion in focus)
Includes index.
ISBN 1-58340-468-6
1. Judaism—Juvenile literature. I. Title. II. Series.

BM573.T44 2004
296—dc22   2003190054

9 8 7 6 5 4 3 2 1

Acknowledgments
Thank you to Rabbi Margaret Jacobi at the Birmingham
Progressive Synagogue for permission to reproduce the pictures on
pages 9b, 17, 21t and 30b

The publishers would also like to thank the following for
permission to reproduce photographs in this book:

J. Arnold/Trip: 24c. Bojan Brecelji/Corbis: 28c. Chris Fairclough
9b, 17, 21t, 30b. I. Genut/Trip: 25t, 26t. Robert Holmes/Corbis:
19t. H.Isachar/Trip: 5c, 29t. E. James/Trip: 15t, 21b. Miki
Kratsman/Corbis: 9t. Richard T. Nowitz/Corbis: 18b. Z.Radovan,
Jerusalem: 4b, 7b, 14b, 23t. H.Rogers/Trip: 6t, 15b, 18t. Steve Shott
Photography cover, 3, 10, 11, 12, 16. A.Tjagny-Rjadno/Trip: 8c. A.
Tovy/Trip: 13b, 22c, 27b.

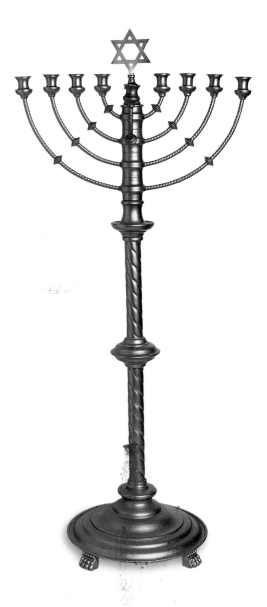

Contents

Origins and history *4*

Jewish beliefs about God *6*

Jewish groups *8*

The Tanakh and the Torah *10*

Jewish values *12*

Shabbat *14*

The synagogue *16*

Family life *18*

High Holy Days and festivals *20*

Sacred places *24*

Life rituals *26*

Key questions and answers *30*

Glossary *31*

Index *32*

Judaism is the religion of the Jews, a group of people who originate from the Middle East. The first Jews were called Hebrews. They were nomads, traveling across what is now called Syria, Israel, and Egypt. Since then, Judaism has spread to countries across the world.

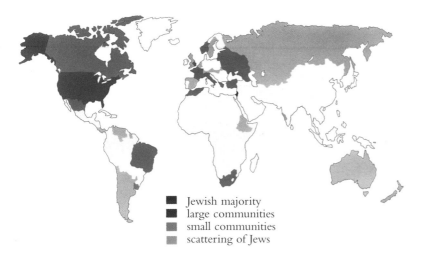

- ■ Jewish majority
- ■ large communities
- ■ small communities
- ■ scattering of Jews

JEWISH POPULATION
There are about 14 million Jews in the world today. Nearly 6 million live in the U.S., 5 million in Israel, and 285,000 in Great Britain.

GOD AND ABRAHAM

Jews believe that about 4,000 years ago, God appeared to their leader, Abraham. God promised that if Abraham and his family lived fair and wise lives, then he would look after them forever and give the Hebrews a land of their own. This was the Promised Land, or Canaan, which Jews now call Israel.

JACOB AND HIS SONS

Jacob, one of Abraham's grandsons, was also known as Israel. As a result, the people who were descendants of Jacob were called Israelites: the children of Israel. His sons and grandsons led 12 Israelite tribes. They lived in the Promised Land until famine struck and Jacob led them to Egypt, where they settled. After several hundred years, a new Pharaoh forced the Israelites to become slaves.

THE EXODUS
Moses led the Israelites safely across the Red Sea.

MOSES AND THE ARK

Jews believe that God wanted to bring the children of Israel back to the Promised Land. He chose Moses, an Israelite who had been adopted by the Pharaoh's daughter, to lead them out of slavery and across the Red Sea to freedom. This is called the Exodus. When the Israelites reached Mount Sinai, Moses received the *Torah* (*see pages 10–11*) and the 10 Commandments (*see opposite*) from God. The Israelites built a special container for the *Torah,* called the Ark. They traveled with it for 40 years until they reached the Promised Land, just after the death of Moses. In the city of Jerusalem, they eventually built a temple in which they placed the Ark. The Temple became the Jews' holiest place.

THE 10 COMMANDMENTS

The 10 Commandments are 10 rules given to Moses by God that Jews use as a guide for how God wants them to live (*see right*).

EXILE AND THE DIASPORA

In 586 B.C., about 600 years after the Israelites reached Canaan, Jerusalem was attacked by the Babylonians and the Temple was destroyed. The Israelites, who were now called Jews, were sent into exile in Babylon and places even further away. These new settlements became known as the Diaspora (scattering). In 538 B.C., Cyrus, the king of Persia, conquered Babylon and allowed Jews to return to Jerusalem. Some Jews returned to rebuild the Temple.

ROMAN RULE

In 63 B.C., the Jews and their land came under the rule of Rome. Jews split into groups with different ideas about how they should practice Judaism. Many Jews hoped a leader, called the Messiah (King of the Jews), would free them. Some thought that Jesus of Nazareth was the Messiah.

During their rule, the Romans destroyed the second temple in Jerusalem. At one point the Jews rebelled, but they were defeated and many Jews fled again. The Jewish Diaspora developed in different countries around the world, but a small number of Jews continued to live in the land of Israel. In modern times, many Jews returned to Israel because of persecution in Europe. In 1948, after the horrors suffered during the World War II, (*see below*), Jews founded the state of Israel. Today, these Jews (called Israelis) remain in conflict with the Palestinians who have lived in the land for generations.

THE HOLOCAUST

After the defeat of Germany in World War I, the German Nazi Party blamed Jews for their country's problems. Their claims were untrue, but when Adolf Hitler came to power in 1933, the rights of Jews were gradually taken away. The Nazis built brutal concentration camps where Jews and other people who disagreed with the Nazis were imprisoned. During World War II, the Nazis murdered six million Jewish people from many different countries. This terrible act is known as the Holocaust.

THE 10 COMMANDMENTS

1. I am the Lord your God, who brought you out of Egypt, from slavery.
2. Worship no other gods but me.
3. Do not use my name falsely.
4. Keep the *Shabbat* day holy.
5. Respect your father and mother.
6. Do not kill.
7. Do not commit adultery.
8. Do not steal.
9. Do not tell lies about others.
10. Do not be jealous of other people's possessions.

THE CITY OF JERUSALEM

Jerusalem is the capital of Israel. It is a holy city for Jews, Muslims, and Christians.

Most Jews believe God governs everything in the universe. This belief raises questions about the nature of God, how his existence in the world can be proved, and why God allows human suffering.

ETHICAL MONOTHEISM

Judaism is often called a religion of "ethical monotheism." For Jews this means that moral (ethical) values and belief in one God (monotheism) go together. Judaism is both a faith and a way of life—you cannot have one without the other.

The *Shema* prayer (*see left*) sums up Jewish belief about the oneness of God and the need for humans to love God.

THE SHEMA PRAYER

This copy of the Shema prayer is written in Hebrew. It is the most important Jewish prayer and is the one Jews say most often (*see below*).

This is the beginning of the *Shema* (meaning "listen") prayer, which is taken from the book of Deuteronomy in the *Tanakh* (the Jewish holy book—*see pages 10–11*). "Hear O Israel! The Lord our God, the Lord is One. You shall love the Lord your God with all your heart, with all your spirit, and with all your strength."

GOD AS CREATOR

Jews believe that God is the creator and sustainer of the universe. A prayer for Jewish morning service says: "Blessed are You, Lord our God, King of the Universe, who forms light and creates darkness, who makes peace and creates all things." According to the *Tanakh* (*see page 10*), everything that exists or happens in the world depends on God, and "the whole of the Earth is full of God's glory." At the same time, Jews believe that God is transcendent—wholly beyond human reach. However, while God is beyond human beings, Jews believe God is also present for them as a loving, personal force. Many Jews seldom write the word "God." Often they write "G–d." This is out of respect for God's perfection and "otherness." Using someone's name is an indication of knowing them; Jews believe humans cannot fully know God.

PROOF OF GOD'S EXISTENCE

For Jews, proof of God's existence can be found in two main sources. Firstly, Creation itself—the beauty and pattern of nature. Secondly, the experience of God in Jewish life. Jews believe that the *Torah* shows that God has been involved with humanity from the moment humans were created. This is most clearly seen in the symbol of the Ark (*see page 4*) and the covenants made between God and the Jewish people.

GOD'S PROMISE

God's promise is to bless the Jews and maintain a close and caring relationship with them forever. This is difficult for some Jews to understand, given the suffering that they have experienced.

SUFFERING

An example of suffering recorded in the *Tanakh* is the story of Job, a good man who suffers terribly. Job's suffering leads him to challenge God as to why such suffering should happen to him. God replies: "Where were you when I created the world?" This suggests that human understanding is too limited to see how suffering fits into the pattern of the universe. The only response is to put faith and trust in God.

But how can God let evil things happen? The biggest challenge to belief in God for many Jews is the Holocaust. Because of the Holocaust, some Jews feel that it is impossible to believe in God. But most regard the events of that period as an extreme example of human evil.

HUMAN NATURE—THE BALANCE OF GOOD AND EVIL

Jews view human nature as made up of *yetzer haTov* (good inclination) and *yetzer haRa* (evil inclination). These inclinations are equally balanced, and people have the ability (free will) to choose one or the other. Humanity has the task of overcoming the many evils in the world. This is known as "repairing the world," or *tikkun olam* in Hebrew. All humans should regard their good deeds as pushing the world's balance toward good, and their bad deeds as pushing the world toward evil.

BIRKHOT HANEHENIN
Blessings of the senses are said by Jews before and after eating. Jews thank God in this way for many things.

BLESSINGS

Despite human suffering, Jewish people are thankful to God. This is most obviously shown each day in the form of blessings. There are many different types of blessings, but the most regular are known as *birkhot hanehenin* (blessings of the senses). These are said before and after eating, on seeing beautiful things in nature, such as a rainbow; on meeting a learned person, and on many other occasions. One

tradition is that a person should say a hundred blessings a day, and most Jews believe this is not difficult as there are so many signs of God's goodness for which to be thankful.

Jewish groups

AN ASHKENAZI JEW
Traditionally, Ashkenazi Jews speak Yiddish. Their name originates from Germany.

Most Jews have a strong sense of identity built up through a long history of discrimination and suffering. This is one of the things that binds Jews together as a people. Jews also share a common language. Although many have another language as their first tongue, they all use Hebrew (spoken by the ancient Jews) for prayer, study, and education.

GEOGRAPHICAL DIFFERENCES

There have been Jewish communities in many parts of the world since 586 B.C. Today, there are two main geographical groups—Sefardi and Ashkenazi, which take their names from the Hebrew for "Spain" and "Germany" respectively. The differences between them lie in customs rather than ideas. For example, Sefardi Jews originally spoke a language called Ladino, which came from Spanish, while the traditional tongue of the Ashkenazi Jews is Yiddish, which developed from medieval German.

IDEOLOGICAL DIFFERENCES

Jews from all geographical groups have different ideas about the meaning of their religion, and how they should practice it. There are two main Jewish groups, as well as some people who are Jewish but do not actively practice their religion.

ORTHODOX JEWS

Orthodox Jews believe Moses received the complete *Torah*; it is a direct account of the word of God. They live by the *Torah*, even when the meaning is hard to understand. About 60 percent of Jews in Great Britain are Orthodox, compared to less than 10 percent in the United States.

One particular Orthodox movement is called Hasidim (pious ones). The movement began in the 18th century in eastern and central Europe. The leaders of the Hasidic movement are known as *tzaddikim* and are often seen as a bridge between humanity and God. Some Hasidic men wear fur hats, boys have short hair with long side locks, and married women may wear wigs or headscarves.

HASIDIC JEWS
Hasidic Judaism is an Orthodox movement.

PROGRESSIVE JEWS

Progressive Jews believe that the *Torah* was written down over many centuries. They accept that it is inspired by God but feel that it can be interpreted to fit modern times. Progressive Jews look for the principles of the *Torah*, rather than taking it literally. They also use more English in their prayer books and worship. In Great Britain only about 20 to 25 percent of Jews are Progressive, while in the U.S. the figure is about 20 percent.

There are different groups of Progressive Jews. Reform Jews and Liberal Jews believe that Judaism must respond to change, as the modern world is very different from Biblical times. The Liberal movement was started in 1902. Liberal Jews emphasize practices and beliefs that have clear reasons; for example, the food laws should be kept because they help a person to think about what they eat.

Conservative Jews are not Progressive Jews, but they also believe that Judaism should respond to change. They tend to have more traditional practices than Progressive Jews. In Great Britain, Conservative Judaism is called Masorti, which means "traditional."

PROGRESSIVE JEWS
There are different groups of Progressive Jews, including Reform and Liberal Jews.

The Tanakh and the Torah

The Hebrew Bible has three sections: *Torah*, *Nevi'im*, and *Ketuvim*. It is given the name *Tanakh*, which is based on the initial letters of the three words.

Nevi'im includes historical books and the writings of the prophets. *Ketuvim* (writings) includes Psalms, Proverbs, and the Song of Songs. The most complex of the three parts is the *Torah*.

WHAT IS THE TORAH?

The word *Torah* means instruction or teaching. It is the basis of Jewish belief and practice. The *Torah* contains the story of God's role in history, and most importantly, instructions for how God wants people to live. These are called commandments (*mitzvot*).

There are two definitions of *Torah*. The narrow definition refers just to the "five books of Moses": *Genesis*, *Exodus*, *Leviticus*, *Numbers,* and *Deuteronomy*. These contain early Jewish history and commandments, and teachings covering every aspect of human existence—relationships with God, with other people, and with the Earth. Running parallel with this, to make up the broader definition, is the oral *Torah*—teachings and interpretations of the written word. They were originally passed on by word of mouth, but have been written down for about 2,000 years.

Different Jewish groups have different views on both the written and oral *Torah*. Orthodox Jews see the written *Torah* as the revealed word of God and the oral *Torah* as reliable interpretations, originally by Moses, and handed down to his successors. Reform Jews believe that both the written and oral *Torah* developed according to history and culture, although they do see the written *Torah* as inspired by God.

THE TORAH SCROLLS
Each *Torah* scroll contains the five books of Moses. The scrolls are covered with beautiful material and decorated with silver ornaments.

PRACTICES CONNECTED WITH THE TORAH

There are a variety of practices connected with the *Torah* that show its importance in Jewish life:

- Jews are encouraged to study the *Torah* regularly. Children study it from about five years of age at *heder*—a school normally attached to a synagogue (a Jewish place of worship—*see pages 16–17*).

- Regular reading from the *Torah* is a central part of synagogue services.

- The *Torah* is kept in a large cupboard called the Ark. The scrolls (there is usually more than one *Torah* in the synagogue) are ornately decorated with beautiful material and silver ornaments.

- Before and after a reading, the scrolls are paraded around the synagogue. They are kissed with the fringe of the *tallit* (prayer shawl) while parading and before reading.

- Worshipers always stand for the procession and for certain readings. Sefardi Jews lift up the scroll before reading (*see right*), and Ashkenazi Jews after reading, to show its high status.

- Each year, at the end of the festival of *Sukkot* (*see page 22*), Jews celebrate *Simhat Torah*. The term means "rejoicing in the *Torah*." During the morning and evening services, the scrolls are taken around the synagogue, accompanied by lively dancing and singing.

READING THE TORAH
Reading the *Torah* is a central part of the synagogue service. It is read using a pointer. This is one way that Jews show their respect for the holy text.

GOD'S COMMANDMENTS (MITZVOT)

A very important aspect of the *Torah* is that Jews believe it reveals how God wants people to live. This means living a life of holiness according to all of God's commandments (*mitzvot*), the individual instructions from God. Traditionally, there are said to be 613 *mitzvot*. Some of these are stated in a positive way—things people should do (e.g. feed the hungry), and some in a negative way—things people should not do (e.g. do not steal). Also, some *mitzvot* are to do with relationships between people (e.g. visit the sick, help those in need, comfort those in mourning), while other *mitzvot* govern relationships between people and God. These include putting a *mezuzah* on the door (*see page 18*), adult males wearing *tefillin* (*see page 13*) on weekdays, observing *Shabbat* (*see pages 14–15*), and observing the laws of *kashrut* (*see pages 18–19*). In one interpretation, the 613 *mitzvot* are divided into 365 negative (to correspond to the days of the year) and 248 positive (to correspond to the parts of the human body). The *mitzvot* govern every aspect of human existence.

Judaism is not just about believing in God and the *Torah*. It is also about applying this belief to everyday life and obeying the *mitzvot*. This forms part of the Jewish law, called *Halacha*.

Halacha enables Jews to bring the holiness of God, or *kedusha*, into their everyday lives. Studying the *Torah* and keeping the *mitzvot* leads to a way of life in which certain values of love, justice, and holiness are important. These values reflect the strong Jewish belief that it is humanity's task to overcome many evils and repair the world (*see page 7*).

LOVE

The first value is love. This is written in the *Torah* as the "golden rule": "you shall love your neighbor as yourself" *(Leviticus 19: 18)*. It is also expressed in an old Hasidic saying: "To love God truly, one must first love

humanity. And if anyone claims to love God and does not love people, you may be sure it is a lie." God's love for creation and humanity is mentioned constantly in the *Torah* and in prayers. God is often called *haRahaman*, which means "the compassionate one."

The *Shema* (*see page 6*) emphasizes that in return for God's love, people should love God. Jews believe that even if a feeling of love does not exist, then the practice of acting in a loving way will enable love to grow. In Hebrew, the name for loving actions is *gemilut hasadim*. This can involve providing meals for the needy, visiting the sick, and volunteering at summer camps for disadvantaged children.

CHILDREN'S PLAYGROUP
Jews regard working for charity as an act of justice. Many Jews devote time to looking after children.

JUSTICE

Justice is a very important value in Jewish life. Much of the *Halacha* is concerned with bringing justice into the world. For Jews, one very important aspect of justice is sharing things fairly, known as *tzedakah* (charity). Therefore, giving to charity is seen as an act of justice rather than kindness. People who have more than they need are expected to donate money and time to other people who are less fortunate.

HOLINESS

According to the book of Leviticus (19: 1), God said to Moses: "Say to all the congregation of the people of Israel, You shall be holy; for I the Lord your God am holy." Holiness is very important for Jews. They use the word *kedusha*, which means "separate or distinct," to refer to the holiness of God. Humans cannot fully know God, but they can develop certain attitudes and behavior that can bring some of God's holiness into the world. Examples of this include performing actions lovingly, praying regularly, and reciting blessings.

There are many symbolic reminders of God's holiness for Jews. These include the *tallit* (prayer shawl) and *tefillin*. *Tefillin* are two black leather boxes containing words from the *Torah*, worn by Orthodox Jewish men. One is bound to the forehead and the other to the left arm, next to the heart. The *tallit* and *tefillin* are worn during prayer. Other symbols of God's holiness include *mezuzah* (*see page 18*) and *kasher* food (*see pages 18–19*).

A JEWISH MAN WEARING THE TALLIT AND TEFILLIN
During prayer on weekday mornings, Orthodox Jewish men wear the *tallit* and *tefillin*. These are symbolic reminders of God's holiness.

13

Shabbat

Shabbat (the Sabbath) is celebrated at home by Jews every week.

THE MEANING OF SHABBAT

Jews believe it is important to bring the holiness of God (*kedusha*) into everyday life. One way they do this is to make time holy, or sacred, by keeping the Sabbath. The commandment to keep the Sabbath occurs twice in the *Torah*, in Exodus and Deuteronomy. In Exodus, *Shabbat* is connected with the seventh day of Creation, when God created a day of rest and relaxation. In Deuteronomy, *Shabbat* is linked to the freedom from slavery in Egypt. Therefore, *Shabbat* commemorates the creation of the universe by God and challenges Jewish people to think about what are the important things in life. A famous rabbi, Hugo Gryn, once said: "*Shabbat* teaches us that while we may own our possessions, our possessions do not own us." This means that although everyday work and earning money have their place, they must not take over a person's life. Time for each other and time for God are more important.

LIGHTING THE SHABBAT CANDLES

The *Shabbat* candles are lit on Friday before sunset. The mother spreads her hands over the candles to welcome the warmth and peace of *Shabbat*.

SHABBAT CELEBRATIONS

FRIDAY EVENING

Shabbat begins before sunset on Friday evening and finishes at nightfall on Saturday. On Friday the home is cleaned, any remaining shopping is done, and food is prepared for the three meals eaten during *Shabbat*. Then family members wash and change into clean clothes. About half an hour before the sun sets, the mother and children light the *Shabbat* candles. They are lit before sunset because the *Torah* forbids the lighting of fire on the Sabbath. The mother draws her hands around the lit candles three to seven times, moving them up towards her face in a symbolic gesture. Then she covers her eyes with her hands and says: "Blessed are You, Lord our God, King of the universe, who has sanctified us with His commandments and commanded us to light the *Shabbat* candles." Other members of the family attend the synagogue for a short service on Friday evening. When they return, the greetings "*Gut Shabbos*" or "*Shabbat Shalom*" are exchanged and a passage from the book of Proverbs is read. Any children present receive a blessing.

THE SHABBAT MEAL

A prayer ritual called *Kiddush* (*see page 17*) is carried out over a full glass of wine to symbolize the joy of *Shabbat*. Afterwards, everyone washes their hands and two *hallah* loaves are uncovered. The cover symbolizes the dew on the ground when God gave the Jews manna (holy bread) in the desert. There are two loaves to symbolize the double portion of manna found on Fridays so that Jews would not have to gather it on *Shabbat*. Traditionally the bread is broken, sprinkled with salt, and passed around the table. The Friday night meal then follows, which is considered the best meal of the week. It is often the one time when the whole family gets together. Sometimes guests are invited to share in this happy occasion. Songs are also sung in many homes.

SATURDAY

In the morning many Jews attend a *Shabbat* service in the synagogue (*see page 17*). When the family returns, *Kiddush* is carried out and

traditional songs are sung, followed by a meal. The afternoon may be spent in study, conversation, or walking with the family. *Shabbat* finishes just after nightfall, with a ceremony called *Havdalah*. A plaited candle is lit, which symbolizes the three themes of *Shabbat*: God, the *Torah,* and Israel. Blessings are said over wine and spices and then the candle is put out with a drop of wine. In this way it is hoped that the sweet smell of *Shabbat* will influence the early days of the week before preparation begins for the next *Shabbat*.

KIDDUSH
Before the *Shabbat* meal, the father says a blessing over a full glass of wine to give thanks for *Shabbat*.

HAVDALAH CANDLE
The plaited candle symbolizes the three themes of *Shabbat*.

15

A RABBI IN A SYNAGOGUE
A rabbi is a Jewish teacher and leader. He or she helps people to understand the meaning of the *Torah*.

Jews meet, pray, and study in a building called a synagogue (meeting place). It is also known by other names that reflect the main purposes of the building. These are: *Bet Tefillah* (house of prayer) and *Bet Knesset* (house of meeting). A synagogue may also have a *Bet Midrash* (house of study).

Orthodox and Progressive synagogues are different. In the prayer hall of an Orthodox synagogue, men and women sit separately, often with the women in a gallery upstairs. Men wear the *tallit* (prayer shawl) and, in both Orthodox and Progressive synagogues, the *kippah* (headcovering). In Progressive synagogues, all people sit together. Also, the *bimah* (the desk from which the *Torah* is read) is at the front, whereas in Orthodox synagogues it is usually in the middle.

THE RABBI

Most synagogues have a rabbi. The rabbi is a teacher of the *Torah* and helps to explain its meaning. All rabbis also offer personal and spiritual advice. Orthodox rabbis are always men, but Progressive Jews have both male and female rabbis. In some synagogues there may also be a cantor, or *hazzan*, who leads the prayers throughout most of the service.

SHABBAT SERVICE

The most important service of the week is the *Shabbat* (the Sabbath) service. In Orthodox synagogues this can take up to three hours and includes prayers and readings from the appropriate part of the *Torah*. After Morning Prayer, the *Aron haKodesh* (Ark of the Covenant) is opened and the *Torah* scrolls are taken out and paraded around the synagogue to the *bimah*. The congregation stands as the scrolls are carried. The reading for the week is chanted and seven members of the congregation are called up to recite blessings before and after each section of the reading. This is regarded as an honor and is called *aliyah* (going up).

KIDDUSH

After the *Shabbat* service, *Kiddush* is held in a hall in the synagogue. It reflects the idea of the synagogue being *Bet Knesset*, the house of meeting. Some verses are sung from the *Torah*, which tell about the keeping of *Shabbat*. Then a blessing is said, often by the rabbi, over a glass of wine and everyone has a drink of wine along with cake and cookies. Lively conversation takes place and any visitors are welcomed. If a family is celebrating a special event, such as the birth of a baby, they may provide the wine and food.

Jews often meet at the synagogue at other times during the week to take part in social or educational groups. People also come to visit the rabbi for personal advice.

CHILDREN AT THE HEDER
Children at the *heder* learn about Jewish stories and prayers.

HEDER

The third aspect of the synagogue is *Bet Midrash*, the house of study. Because study of the *Torah* is an essential way of bringing God's holiness into the world, Jewish communities set up *hedarim* (singular: *heder*) or "religion schools." *Hedarim* are usually attached to the synagogue. Children normally go to *heder* at the age of five and continue up to the age of *Bar* or *Bat Mitzvah* (*see pages 26–27*) or older.

Family life

The family and the home are very much at the center of Jewish life. This is because Jews see the family as the most important way of maintaining and passing on their history and values. Two things that identify a Jewish home are the *mezuzah* (plural: *mezuzot*) and *kashrut*.

THE MEZUZAH

Many Jews reach up and touch the *mezuzah* when they enter a room.

MEZUZAH

The *mezuzah* is a small box containing a piece of parchment that is nailed to the right-hand doorpost of each door in the house. On the parchment is a verse from the book of Deuteronomy (6: 9). It says: "And you shall write [these words] on the doorpost of your house and gates." The verse refers to the words of the *Shema* (*see page 6*). Written on the back of the parchment is the word *Shaddai* (Almighty). It is also said to stand for the initial letters of *Shomer Daltot Yisrael* (the Guardian of the Doors of Israel). In this sense the *mezuzah* represents the protection of the household by God.

Many Jews reach up and touch the *mezuzah* when they enter the house or a room in the house. This is to remind them that they should live their lives according to the words contained inside.

KASHRUT

For Orthodox families it is extremely important to keep the laws of *kashrut* (fitness). Reform or Liberal families keep the laws to different degrees, and there are some Jews who do not keep them at all.

PREPARING HALLAH BREAD

All Jewish bread is prepared according to the laws of *kashrut*. *Hallah* bread is specially braided and is eaten at *Shabbat* and during some festivals.

LAWS OF KASHRUT

The basic laws of *kashrut* can be found in Chapter 11 of Leviticus. The first group of rules is about what foods are considered to be *kasher* (also spelled *kosher*, meaning "fit" or "proper," from the word *kashrut*). *Kasher* foods are: all plants, fruits, and vegetables; mammals with split hooves and which chew the cud (for example, sheep, but not pigs); fish with both scales and fins (for example, cod, but not shellfish); all domestic birds; the milk of any *kasher* mammal; and the eggs of any *kasher* bird. The second set of rules governs the killing of animals for food. Jews kill animals for food by a method they believe to be the most humane—slitting the throat. Stunning an animal first is not allowed and only one cut should be made with a very sharp knife. This ritual slaughter is called *shehitah*, and the person who does it a *shohet*. Jews believe that the "spirit of life" is contained in the blood of all creatures, and so all blood is drained from the meat before it is eaten.

The laws of *kashrut* also include rules about the way in which meat and milk are used. In many Jewish kitchens there are separate sets of cooking utensils, cutlery, and cloths to ensure the rules are kept.

RULES FOR USING MEAT AND MILK

1. Meat and milk must not be cooked together: "You shall not boil a kid in the milk of its mother."

2. Meat and milk products must not be eaten together.

3. Meat and milk must not come into contact with one another.

High Holy Days and festivals

For Jews, time is sacred, and it is very important that they set aside periods throughout the year to remember God in every part of life.

Many Jewish holy days and festivals celebrate different aspects of Jewish life, history, and their relationship with God. The High Holy Days of *Rosh Hashanah* and *Yom Kippur* are celebrated because the *Torah* says that these times should be set apart from everyday life. The pilgrim festivals of *Sukkot*, *Pesach*, and *Shavu'ot*, and such other festivals as *Hanukkah* and *Purim*, are celebrated to remember an important aspect of Jewish life or history.

THE JEWISH YEAR

Jews use a lunar calendar. This means that each month of the year, starting with *Tishri*, begins with a new moon (every 29 or 30 days). This makes the lunar year add up to 354 days. So, every third year a month called *Adar* is added to make sure the High Holy Days and festivals are celebrated at the right time of year. Jewish years are counted from the first *Shabbat* of Creation, which according to Judaism happened in 3760 B.C. So in the year A.D. 2000, for example, Creation happened 5,762 years ago. Progressive Jews accept that the world is much older, as do many modern Orthodox Jews. Both groups believe that Creation marks the beginning of the world as humans understand it.

The Jewish months of the year are:

Tishri	(September/October)
Heshvan	(October/November)
Kislev	(November/December)
Tevet	(December/January)
Sh'vat	(January/February)
Adar	(February/March)
Nisan	(March/April)
Iyyar	(April/May)
Sivan	(May/June)
Tamuz	(June/July)
Av	(July/August)
Elul	(August/September)

HIGH HOLY DAYS OF THE NEW YEAR

ROSH HASHANAH

Rosh Hashanah is celebrated on the first and second of *Tishri* and marks the beginning of the season of repentance, or saying sorry. The Hebrew word for repentance is *teshuvah* (returning). The High Holy Day is linked to three stories in the *Torah*. The first one is the Creation, when God created the world. It is traditional to share pieces of apple dipped in honey at *Kiddush (see page 17)*. This symbolizes the hope of a sweet and happy new year ahead. At *Rosh Hashanah* people also remember that everyone should obey God. The story of Abraham's readiness to sacrifice his son Isaac is an example of this. At the festival, a ram's horn called a *shofar* is blown as a way to remember Abraham's faith. It is also a reminder that Jewish people need to seek repentance.

PREPARING APPLES AND HONEY

Apples and honey are shared at *Rosh Hashanah* to wish for a sweet and happy new year.

YOM KIPPUR

Eight days after *Rosh Hashanah*, Jews observe the Day of Atonement, or *Yom Kippur*. On this day everybody tries to make amends for their sins and seek forgiveness. Many Jews spend the whole day in the synagogue, where five different services of prayer and readings from the *Torah* are held. The synagogue is decorated in white, and many people dress in white. Everyone who observes *Yom Kippur* must fast, unless there are medical reasons for not doing so. At *Yom Kippur* people accept that they make mistakes in their lives and are capable of hurting themselves and others. *Yom Kippur* enables the whole Jewish community to come together. The service and the fast end with a single call of the *shofar*.

THE SHOFAR

The *shofar* is blown for many different reasons. During High Holy Days it reminds Jews that they need to seek repentance. It also marks the end of *Yom Kippur*.

Jews were commanded to go on pilgrimages by the *Torah*: "Three times a year, at *Pesach*, at *Shavu'ot,* and at *Sukkot,* all your males shall appear before the Lord your God in the place that he will choose."
Deuteronomy (16: 16)

FESTIVALS OF THE TORAH

Sukkot, Pesach, and *Shavu'ot* are called pilgrim festivals because they celebrate times when Jewish people were commanded to go on pilgrimages to Jerusalem (*see left*).

SUKKOT

Sukkot is celebrated from the 15th to the 21st (22nd for Orthodox Diaspora) day of *Tishri* (September/October). It marks the end of the harvest, when people traditionally built simple huts in the fields to be near their crops. It also remembers the time when Jewish people were wandering in the desert after the Exodus from Egypt. Another name for *Sukkot* is the Feast of Tabernacles. This name refers to the tents that the nomadic Jews lived in because they did not have permanent homes. Today, at home and at the synagogue during the festival, Jewish people build a temporary shelter called a *sukkah* (plural: *sukkot*). This is usually placed outside. Greenery is draped over the *sukkah* and it is important that the stars can be seen through the roof. This reminds people that life on Earth does not last forever and that God is the most important thing in life. Some Jews live in the *sukkah* during the eight days of the festival. Others just eat their meals there.

A SUKKAH
This *sukkah* has a roof made from palm leaves. This allows the stars to be seen through the roof.

During the morning service in the synagogue, four plants—palm, myrtle, willow, and a yellow citrus fruit called an *etrog*, or citron—are waved in all directions. Jews are told to do this in Leviticus (23: 40), and it is an act of rejoicing before God. The last day of the festival is called *Simhat Torah* (*see page 11*).

HANUKKAH AND PURIM

These two festivals mark important events in Jewish history that the rabbis said should be remembered. *Hanukkah* (dedication) is celebrated from the 25th day of *Kislev* until the third day of *Tevet* (December/January). In 175 B.C., the Syrians attempted to destroy the Temple in Jerusalem. The festival commemorates the deeds of Judah the Maccabee, who defeated them. At *Hanukkah*, Jews light a special lamp called a *menorah* or *hanukkiah*. This holds eight candles to remember the miracle of the oil lamp. Following the reclamation of the Temple by the Jews, there was only enough oil to light it for one day. But, remarkably, the lamp burned for eight days.

Purim is celebrated on the 14th day of *Adar* (around the beginning of March), and commemorates the events recorded in the book of Esther in the Bible. It is a joyful festival celebrating the courage of Queen Esther of Persia and her uncle Mordechai. In the fifth century B.C. they defeated an evil man named Haman, who wanted all Jews killed. The story is told in synagogues, and every time Haman is mentioned the children stamp and hiss and wave rattles called *greggers*.

PESACH (PASSOVER)

Pesach is celebrated from the 15th to the 21st (22nd for Orthodox Diaspora) day of *Nisan* (March/April) and commemorates the Exodus from Egypt. At *Pesach*, Jews remember that God set the Jewish nation free and chose them to be his people. In Israel the festival lasts for a week, but elsewhere it lasts for eight days. The main celebration is the Seder meal, at which each family retells the story of the Exodus. Unleavened bread (made without yeast), called *matzah*, is eaten because during the Exodus the Jews did not have time to let their bread rise. Before *Pesach* begins, all products containing yeast are cleared from the house. The Seder meal is full of symbolism, especially the Seder plate, on which certain symbolic foods are placed.

THE SEDER MEAL
The Seder meal occurs during *Pesach*. It celebrates the Exodus from Egypt.

FOODS ON THE SEDER PLATE

A roasted egg and roasted shankbone of lamb—represent sacrifices made to God in the Temple.

Bitter herbs—eaten to recall the bitterness of slavery.

Charoset—a mixture made from apples, nuts, cinnamon, and wine—eaten to symbolize the mortar that Israelite slaves made in Egypt.

A green vegetable—symbolizes the coming of spring and new life.

A dish of salty water—reminds Jews of the tears shed by the slaves.

SHAVU'OT

Shavu'ot is celebrated on the sixth day of Sivan (May/June), but Orthodox Diaspora also celebrate it on the seventh. It commemorates God giving the *Torah* to Moses on Mount Sinai. At *Shavu'ot*, synagogues are decorated with greenery and flowers, and the 10 Commandments are read during worship. On the night before the festival, many Jews stay awake, reading and discussing the *Torah*. A special meal is eaten that includes foods made of milk and honey. This reminds people of the vow made by God to Moses, that the Promised Land would be flowing with milk and honey. Often, honey sweets are given to a child when he or she begins to learn the *Torah*.

Today, Jews do not have to make pilgrimages (religious journeys), but many like to visit holy places in Israel.

ISRAEL

The land of Israel, with Jerusalem at its center, is very important to Jews. It is a small country, but it has a landscape that ranges from sandy shores to snow-capped mountains. Many religions are represented in Israel, including Christianity, Islam, Baha'i, Samaritanism, and various branches of Judaism. For Jews, Israel is a sacred place, first promised to Abraham by God. In Genesis (17: 7–8) God says to Abraham: "I will maintain my covenant between me and you and your offspring to come. . . . I give the land you stay in to you and your offspring to come, all the land of Canaan, as an everlasting possession." The *Amidah*, a prayer that is said three times a day, includes prayers for the return of Israel and the rebuilding of Jerusalem. At the end of festivals such as *Pesach* people say, "Next year in Jerusalem." Many Jews still live outside Israel, and they visit to feel close to their traditions and religion.

THE WESTERN WALL

The Western Wall in Jerusalem is the holiest Jewish place. It is all that remains of the Temple.

THE WESTERN WALL

The holiest Jewish place is the Western Wall in Jerusalem, also known as the wailing wall. It is the remains of the Temple built by King Herod in 29 B.C. Traditionally, Jews visit it to mourn the destruction of the Temple. The Western Wall is a favorite place for *Bar Mitzvah* ceremonies (*see pages 26–27*). These are held on Mondays, Thursdays, and *Shabbat* because these are the days when the *Torah* is read. Some visitors write prayers on pieces of paper and put them in the cracks between the stones in the wall. Today, no matter where Jews are in the world, when they pray together they face in the direction in which the Temple once stood in Jerusalem.

YAD VASHEM

Yad Vashem is a memorial to Jewish people who died in the Holocaust (*see page 5*). One of the main purposes of Yad Vashem is to make sure that no one forgets the horrors that Jews suffered. The world's largest collection of material about the Holocaust is found there, including 58 million pages of documents and about 100,000 photographs. In the Hall of Remembrance, a light burns constantly. In front of the flame lies a crypt, which contains the ashes of some of the victims. On the floor are the names of some of the Nazi concentration camps where Jews were murdered or died. There is also a special garden, called "The Garden of the Righteous Among the Nations," where trees have been planted in memory of the non-Jewish people who risked their lives to save Jews during the Holocaust. In the Hall of Names there are symbolic gravestones, called "Pages of Testimony," which list the names and details of people who died. Jewish people did not want to remember the victims just as identification numbers, so families, friends, and neighbors have been encouraged to supply information. So far, 3.2 million names have been entered in the computer at Yad Vashem.

CHILDREN'S MEMORIAL AT YAD VASHEM

This is a memorial at Yad Vashem to more than one million children who died during the Holocaust.

A BABY BOY IS PREPARED FOR BRIT MILAH

Brit Milah is a permanent sign that a boy is part of the agreement made between God and Abraham.

Judaism, like all major world religions, has a number of rituals and celebrations. These mark significant stages in a Jew's life and the role that God plays in it.

BRIT MILAH

Brit Milah (covenant of circumcision) is a sign of the agreement made between God and Abraham *(Genesis 17: 10–11)*. The ceremony must take place on the eighth day after the birth of a baby boy. It can be carried out at home, in the hospital, or in a synagogue. It is usually performed by a *mohel*, a person trained in the *Halacha* (law) and medical hygiene. It is the father's responsibility to see that the circumcision is carried out. Traditionally, the mother is not in the room at the time, although among some Progressive Jews she may be present and even share in some of the ritual.

After the circumcision, the baby is given a Hebrew name. This is followed by a simple meal that gathers all generations of the family together.

A GIRL'S NAMING CEREMONY

In Orthodox communities, on the *Shabbat* immediately after the birth of a daughter, the father is called up to read the *Torah* in the synagogue. Prayers are said for the mother and baby, and the name of the girl is announced. Progressive synagogues hold a similar ceremony on Friday night or *Shabbat* morning.

BAR OR BAT MITZVAH

Bar Mitzvah (son of the commandment) and *Bat Mitzvah* (daughter of the commandment) mark the time when a young person becomes responsible for fulfilling the *mitzvot* (commandments). The ceremonies are connected with the *Torah*.

A boy's *Bar Mitzvah* is held as soon as possible after his 13th birthday. During a synagogue service, the boy is called up to read the *Torah*, and may also lead some parts of the morning prayer. Afterwards, a special meal is held and the boy may give a *D'var Torah*, a commentary on some words of the *Torah*.

A girl's *Bat Mitzvah* takes place when she is 12 years old. This ceremony does not usually include reading from the *Torah* in the synagogue. This reflects the Orthodox view that the roles of men and women are equal, but different. Progressive Jews tend not to make a distinction between how a *Bar* or *Bat Mitzvah* is celebrated.

A BOY READS AT HIS BAR MITZVAH
A *Bar* or *Bat Mitzvah* marks the time when a young person becomes responsible for fulfilling the *mitzvot*.

MARRIAGE

For Jews, marriage is regarded as holy. Jewish weddings can take place out in the open, at home, or in a synagogue. Some couples fast on the day of the wedding until after the ceremony. On the *Shabbat* before the wedding, the bridegroom may be called upon to read from the *Torah*. Afterwards, the people present may call out "*mazal tov*," which means "good luck." In some synagogues, raisins or sweets are thrown to symbolize good wishes.

THE WEDDING DAY

On the wedding day, the bride and her attendants wait in a special room in the synagogue and are visited there by the groom. He recites a blessing to his bride to be: "O sister, be the mother of thousands and ten thousands." He then places a veil over her face, which remains covered until after the ceremony. The ceremony itself takes place under a *huppah*. This is a canopy made of wood, decorated with flowers, and with embroidered cloth stretched over it. It symbolizes the couple's new home. Blessings are recited by the rabbi, and a cup of wine is shared between the bride and groom. The groom places an unadorned ring on the index finger of the bride's right hand and says: "Behold, you are betrothed to me with this ring, according to the law of Moses and of Israel." By accepting the ring, the bride agrees to the marriage.

A JEWISH WEDDING, JERUSALEM

The *ketuba* is read to remind the couple of their responsibilities. The wedding often takes place outside, under a *huppah*.

A document called the *ketuba*, which is often highly decorated, is read to remind the couple of their responsibilities to each other. Two witnesses sign it, and the bride keeps it as proof of the marriage. After this, seven blessings are chanted over a full cup of wine, which is then shared by the bride and groom. Finally, a wineglass is wrapped in a cloth and broken under the groom's foot. This symbolizes the fragile and precious nature of human life.

DEATH

Jews believe there is life after death. However, it is important for a Jewish person to serve God in this life, because the way he or she behaves in this life determines what happens to him or her after death.

Orthodox Jews do not practice cremation because they believe in physical resurrection, when the soul is restored to the body. Some Reform and Liberal Jews do practice cremation, but burial is more common.

When someone dies, the body is washed ritually. This is carried out by members of the *hevra kadisha* (holy society). Although Jews believe the soul leaves the body at death, the body is still respected. Members of the *hevra kadisha* take it in turns to stay with the body from the moment of death until the burial. After washing, the body is dressed in a white shroud and placed in a coffin. Men are normally buried in a shroud and wrapped in their prayer shawl. One of the fringes is cut off to signify the passing away.

Most Jewish communities have their own cemetery, which is either self-contained or a separate section of a public cemetery. There is usually a small prayer house. Part of the funeral service is held in the prayer house and part by the side of the grave. After the coffin has been lowered into the grave, every person helps to put in some earth. This reminds the mourners of the reality of death. They chant the words, "may he/she come to his/her place in peace."

A JEWISH CEMETERY
After death, most Jews are buried in a cemetery. People visiting the grave of a friend or relative often leave a stone as a token on the tomb. People do not leave flowers in a Jewish cemetery.

MOURNING

Mourning begins once the funeral has taken place. Friends of the mourners prepare a meal with special foods. Eggs, for example, are eaten as a symbol of life and fertility. Eggs are also a symbol of the cycle of life and death because they are round in shape. The first week after the funeral is known as *shiva*. The family stays at home and friends come to visit to offer comfort, share grief, or just sit quietly. Visitors may also bring food or do the shopping. After the week of mourning is over, the family returns to everyday life, but family members do not go to parties or to other celebrations until 30 days after the funeral. If the mourning is for a father or mother, then it lasts for another 11 months.

Key questions and answers

WHAT IS JUDAISM? Judaism is the religion of the Jews, a group of people who originate from the Middle East.

HOW MANY JEWS ARE THERE WORLDWIDE? Approximately 14 million.

WHAT JEWISH GROUPS ARE THERE? Sefardi, Ashkenazi, Orthodox (including Hasidic Jews), Progressive Jews (including Reform and Liberal Jews), and Conservative Jews, (*see pages 8–9*).

WHAT DO JEWS BELIEVE? Jews believe that God governs, creates, and sustains the universe. Proof of God's existence can be found in the beauty and pattern of nature, and the experience of God in Jewish life (*see pages 6–7*). The *Torah* reveals how God wants people to live, and it forms the basis of Jewish belief and practice. The *Shema* prayer sums up Jewish belief about God (*see page 6*).

WHAT ARE THE JEWISH TEACHINGS AND VALUES?
Jews follow the teachings in the *Tanakh* (the Hebrew Bible), which is divided into three sections: *Torah*, *Nevi'im,* and *Ketuvim* (*see pages 10–11*). Jews apply this to everyday life through a part of Jewish law called *Halacha* (*see pages 12–13*). Jews believe it is humanity's responsibility to repair the universe through the values of love, justice, and holiness.

WHAT ARE THE JEWISH RULES FOR LIVING?
The 10 Commandments are 10 rules by which Jews live their lives (*see page 5*). Jews also follow the commandments (*mitzvot*) in the *Torah*. These include putting *mezuzot* on doors (*see page 18*), adult males wearing *tefillin* (*see page 13*), observing *Shabbat,* and the laws of *kashrut* (*see pages 18–19*).

WHERE DO JEWS WORSHIP? Jews worship in a synagogue (*see pages 16–17*). Synagogues contain a *bimah*, where the *Torah* is read, and an *Aron haKodesh*, where the *Torah* is kept. Most synagogues have a rabbi.

WHAT ARE THE JEWISH HIGH HOLY DAYS AND FESTIVALS?
High Holy Days: *Rosh Hashanah, Yom Kippur.* Festivals: *Sukkot, Hanukkah, Purim, Pesach,* and *Shavu'ot.*

Glossary

ABRAHAM   The father of the Jewish people who made a covenant with God.

ARK   (*Aron haKodesh*) A special cupboard in the synagogue in which the *Torah* scrolls are kept. It is also the name given to the special container used to keep the 10 Commandments safe during the Exodus.

BAR MITZVAH   (son of the commandment) A ceremony in which a 13-year-old boy becomes fully responsible for fulfilling the *mitzvot*.

BAT MITZVAH   (daughter of the commandment) A ceremony in which a 12-year-old girl becomes fully responsible for fulfilling the *mitzvot*.

BIMAH   The raised platform in a synagogue used for reading the *Torah*.

COVENANT   An agreement made between God and the Jews.

DIASPORA   The scattering of Jews.

EXODUS   The period of 40 years after leaving slavery in Egypt during which the Jews survived in the desert before reaching the Promised Land.

FASTING   Going without food and water.

HALACHA   Jewish laws that enable Jews to bring *kedusha* into their everyday lives.

HAVDALAH   The ceremony held on Saturday night that concludes *Shabbat*.

HEBREW   The language of the Jewish holy books, and also of modern Israel.

HEDER   (plural: *Hedarim*) A Jewish school that is usually attached to a synagogue.

HOLOCAUST   The period during the 1940s when the Nazis murdered millions of Jews.

JERUSALEM   The capital city of Israel which is sacred to Jews, Muslims, and Christians.

KASHER   Food acceptable in Jewish law is described as *kasher* or *kosher*.

KASHRUT   Meaning "fitness." Jewish laws that govern food type, preparation, and consumption.

KEDUSHA   The distinct holiness of God.

KETUVIM   Part of the *Tanakh* that includes Psalms (sacred songs, poems, and prayers), Proverbs (short sayings), and the Song of Songs (dramatic love poems, also called Song of Solomon).

KIDDUSH   The prayers said for *Shabbat* over a cup of wine.

MITZVOT   The commandments found in the *Torah*. It is said that there are 613 *mitzvot,* which govern every part of human existence.

MOSES   The Israelite chosen by God to lead the Jews from Egypt to the Promised Land.

NER TAMID   A permanent light found in the synagogue, in front of the Ark, to show that God is ever-present.

NEVI'IM   Part of the *Tanakh* that includes historical books and the writings of the prophets.

PROMISED LAND   Also called "Canaan." Land promised to Abraham by God.

RABBI   A Jewish teacher and spiritual leader.

SEDER   A special meal eaten during *Pesach,* when families retell the story of the Exodus.

SHABBAT   The Sabbath (held from Friday evening to Saturday evening). The Jewish day of rest and prayer.

SHEMA   A prayer that sums up Jewish belief about the oneness of God and the need for humans to love God.

SHOFAR   A ram's horn blown on Jewish High Holy Days.

SYNAGOGUE   A building in which Jews meet and worship.

TALLIT   A prayer shawl worn in the synagogue.

TANAKH   The Hebrew Bible, which consists of three sections: *Torah*, *Nevi'im* and *Ketuvim*.

TEFILLIN   Two black leather boxes containing words from the *Torah*. One is strapped on the forehead, the other on the left arm during prayer.

TEMPLE   The ancient Jewish temple in Jerusalem. It was the holiest building for the Jews.

TORAH   The holiest teachings of the Jews. The *Torah* is part of the *Tanakh*.

Index

Abraham 4, 21, 24, 26, 31
Ark, the (*Aron haKodesh*) 4, 6, 11, 17, 30, 31

Bar Mitzvah 17, 24, 26–27, 31
Bat Mitzvah 17, 26–27, 31
bimah 16, 17, 30, 31
blessings 7, 13, 15, 17, 28
   birkhot hanehenin (blessings of the senses) 7
Brit Milah 26

Canaan *see Promised Land, the*
commandments *see* mitzvot
Creation 6, 14, 20, 21

Diaspora, the 5, 22, 23, 31

Egypt 4, 5, 14, 22, 23, 31
ethical monotheism 6
Exodus 4, 22, 23, 31

fasting 21, 28, 31
festivals 20, 22–23
   Hanukkah 20, 22, 30
   Pesach 20, 22, 23, 24, 30, 31
   Purim 20, 22–23, 30
   Shavu'ot 20, 22, 23, 30
   Sukkot 11, 20, 22, 30
food 7, 23, 29
food laws *see* kashrut, *laws of*

Great Britain 4, 9

Halacha 12, 26, 30, 31
Hallah bread 15, 18
Havdalah 15, 31
Hebrew 6, 7, 8, 12, 21, 26, 31
heder 11, 17, 31
High Holy Days 20–21
   Rosh Hashanah 20, 21, 30
   Yom Kippur 20, 21, 30
Holocaust, the 5, 7, 25, 31
human nature 7
   yetzer haRa (evil inclination) 7
   yetzer haTov (good inclination) 7
huppah 28

Israel 4, 5, 6, 13, 15, 18, 23, 24, 28, 31
Israelites 4, 23, 31

Jacob 4
Jerusalem 4, 5, 22, 24, 28, 31
Jesus of Nazareth 5
Jewish calendar 20
Jewish groups 8
   Ashkenazi Jews 8, 11, 30
   Conservative Jews 9, 30
   Orthodox Jews 9, 10, 13, 16, 17, 18, 19, 20, 22, 23, 26, 27, 29, 30
      Hasidim 9, 12, 30
   Progressive Jews 9, 16, 17, 20, 26, 27, 30
      Liberal Jews 9, 18, 29, 30
      Reform Jews 9, 10, 18, 29, 30
   Sefardi Jews 8, 11, 30
Jewish population 4, 30
Judah 4, 22

kasher food 13, 18, 19, 31
kashrut (fitness), laws of 9, 11, 18–19, 30, 31
kedusha 12, 13, 14, 31
ketuba 28
Kiddush 15, 17, 21, 31
kippah (headcovering) 16
kosher food *see* kasher *food*

matzah bread 23
menorah 22
Messiah, the 5
mezuzah 11, 13, 18, 30
Middle East, the 4, 30
mitzvot (commandments) 10, 11, 12, 26, 27, 30, 31
Moses 4, 9, 10, 13, 21, 23, 28, 31
Mount Sinai 4, 23

ner tamid 13, 31

Palestinians 5
pilgrimages 22, 24
prayer *or* prayers 6, 12, 15, 17, 21, 24, 26, 29, 31
Promised Land, the 4, 5, 23, 31

rabbis 14, 16, 17, 22, 28, 30, 31
Red Sea, the 4
Romans, the 5

Sabbath, the *see* Shabbat
Seder meal 23, 31
Shabbat 5, 11, 14–15, 20, 24, 26, 28, 30, 31
   candles 14
   meal 15
   service 17
Shema prayer, the 6, 12, 18, 30, 31
shofar 21, 31
Simhat Torah 11, 22
slavery 4, 5, 14, 23
suffering 7, 25
sukkah 22
synagogues 11, 14, 15, 16–17, 21, 22, 23, 26, 27, 28, 30, 31
   Bet Knesset 16, 17
   Bet Midrash 16, 17
   Bet Tefillah 16
Syria 4

tallit (prayer shawl) 11, 13, 16, 29, 31
Tanakh, the 6, 7, 10, 30, 31
   Ketuvim 10, 30, 31
   Nevi'im 10, 30, 31
   Torah, the 4, 6, 9, 10–11, 12, 13, 14, 15, 16, 17, 20, 21, 22, 23, 24, 26, 27, 28, 30, 31
tefillin 11, 13, 30, 31
Temple, the 4, 5, 22, 24, 31
10 Commandments, the 4, 5, 23, 30, 31
tikkun olam (repairing the world) 7, 30
Torah, see Tanakh*, the*
Torah scrolls 10, 11, 17, 31

United States 4, 9

values 12–13, 30

Western Wall, the 24
World War II 5

Yad Vashem 25
Yiddish 8